Spirituality
-A Quest-

(Simple Answers to Complex Questions)

First Print 2024

Notion Press Media Pvt Ltd,
#7, Red Cross Road,
Egmore, Chennai, Tamil Nadu 600008,
India

Processed & Printed in India

Spirituality
-A Quest-

Author
Alok Ganguly

Disclaimer

The thoughts, reactions and suggestions given in the book are not a substitute for any medical service, therefore, in any health-related matter, give priority to medical consultation. Through this book, the publisher or the author does not intend to provide any professional advice or instructions to the readers.

Words of Dedication

Through spiritual experience our mind becomes pure, peaceful, and happy, and we find purpose, meaning in our lives. I am hereby sharing my spiritual experiences, which are just a few drops in the vast ocean of spirituality. I would like to dedicate this book to my dear readers who are physically and mentally healthy or who want to be healthy.

I apologize for any errors in my writing or thoughts, I hope my readers will forgive me.

Table of Contents

About Author

Alok Ganguly is a person of Indian origin who belongs to a middle-class family. He resides in Bengaluru, Karnataka, but he was born and brought up in Delhi. He completed his B.Sc., M.Sc. and PGDM(Management) degrees from Delhi. He has been working with different international companies in India, USA and UK for the past 20 years.

Alok's interest in spirituality began in his early life, which led him to find answers to his spiritual questions. This discovery led him to acquire and practice knowledge of vedanta, yoga and meditation. Eventually, he gained some insight and a simple understanding of spirituality from this vast storehouse of knowledge. Through his book "Spirituality-A Quest", Alok aims to share simple and truthful answers to important spiritual questions with his dear readers.

We hope this book will bring the readers calmness, direction and positive motivation..

Preface

This book is an attempt to provide answers for various spirituality topics.

Spiritual life does not have to be pursued in secluded caves or in a remote himalayan valley, nor is it only for extraordinary people with special abilities.

As we begin our spiritual journey, the truth may seem hard to grasp, but we can not only comprehend but also realize the profound truths of Soul(Atma), Karma(Actions), Yoga, Meditation (Dhayan/Sadhana) by using our simple intelligence and self-awareness. This is the sole purpose of writing this book.

Spirituality is an experience that cannot be felt from the outside world or worldly matter. It is the thrill of your journey, inside your body, the effect of which can make you feel happy and satisfied in your daily routine, both physically and mentally.

The body, which is with you, is a unique experience. Of all the 8.4 million living species, only man has the privilege of discovering the mystery of the universe. By observing and understanding it carefully, you can create a unique meaning in your life. As we all know that this body will not be with us forever, and we need to use this body to find out who is immortal if it is not your body. And this path of spiritual discovery will satisfy your life, body and mind.

We should respect our body and live it with an alignment with the soul. This confluence can help in maintaining your health, but it can also provide you with the possibility of making positive changes in yours and others' lives.

The first step of realization is to acknowledge that a being exists beyond the body, which is the Soul(atma).The body is only a vehicle and it is a means for the soul to travel. The new perspective of looking at it, that is given in this book, can give you the ability to see our lives in a new form.

Spirituality is a unique experiance in which we understand the effects of our physical, mental, and spiritual transformations. It gives us the opportunity to understand the entirety and completeness of this life.

Let us embark on a spiritual journey.

Alok Ganguly
adhyatmik.harisevak@gmail.com

1

Soul(Atma)

1. What is Soul?
2. What is the nature of the Soul?
3. How to identify the Soul?
4. What is the relationship between Soul and God?
5. Why should one try to attain the Soul in worldly life?
6. What is meant by purification of the Soul?
7. What is meant by salvation of the Soul?
8. What is the relation between mind and Soul?

In Hindi, Atma, which means soul, spirit, or self. It is derived from the Sanskrit word atman (आत्मन्), which is a key concept in Hinduism, Buddhism, Jainism, and Sikhism.

All the physical elements of nature, including the physical bodies of conscious beings and their sensory and mental functions, can be grouped together, creating an ever-changing physical aspect of the universe. It is called nature, the *soul* is which resides within every being and animates him.

At the mention of the word "Soul(atma)", we worldly human beings have such an impression as if it does not belong to us or as if we do not want to hear or ask anything about it. Or you can also say, will it give me some benefit or not?

All this because worldly men spent their entire lives in fulfilling their physical bodies desires and aspirations. Here we are not talking about renouncing the household life, but while living in a life of suffering, also seeking to achieve the ultimate joy or bliss.

Now tell me, will this body stay with you forever?

Will it obey you?

"No!",

Then how did it happen to "Your" body? And if the "Body" is not yours, who is the "I". Is it the supreme power that sees and remembers everything by becoming "I" or "self"?

When you think deeply, you will understand that you are not connected to the world. The body, senses, mind and intellect are always changing, but you are constant. If you don't understand this, you may believe it as a certain truth. You may say that this connection cannot be severed, but I can tell you that it cannot be preserved. Did you preserve your childhood and youth? Those phases have changed and gone and everything is changing and going all the time without you doing. You should stop thinking that you cannot sever your connection with them. This connection is breaking up by itself without you doing.

I am sure that now you will want to know all those questions about the Atma and their answers.

This whole world, animals and vegetation are created, operated and destroyed by the coordination of consciousness root matter (the five elements – ether, water, air, earth and fire).

The root nature or inanimate nature is always changing. The form of the body that is visible is the root-form. The visible form of the body is inanimate. For example, the living being takes birth in the form of an egg/living species, then as a child, then as a teenager, as a young man and finally as an old man, after leaving his body, he attains supreme abode(Moksha/Salvation) or rebirth.

Now think a little, who is experiencing the different forms and activities of this inert body or inanimate body, and who is watching and remembering all body activities as a spectator.

That unchanging "who" and

"I" is no one but *the soul*.

In this universe, our bodies as well as the entire universe is ever changing and passing away every moment. But the "I" who knows all these changes is the soul or the seer, it always remains the same.

Our physical body is a machine, and its driver is the mind, but *the Soul* is a distant spectator who keeps checking the work being done by both.

Whatever feelings of lust, anger, joy, sorrow, attachment, aversion etc. arise in the mind, this physical body always experiences happiness and sorrow as a result of them. Our body does not try to know the soul (consciousness) and the divine(supreme soul).

Bhagvad Gita says that the soul is neither born nor dies. Unborn, unchanging, everlasting, primary, even when the body is killed, this soul is not killed. Neither weapons can cut it, nor fire can burn it; neither water can wet it, nor can air dry it. Like a person takes off worn clothes and wears new clothes. In the same way, the soul takes off worn out bodies and enters new bodies.

Now you should understand that the eternal pure awareness that unites truth, consciousness and bliss is your true nature, and not the changing and deteriorating inert body. You are not the body; you are the essence within, spirit, divine entity. When you identify yourself with a limited body then you are a mortal; and when you identify yourself with the soul, then you are immortal.

The brain's intangible functions are not the same as the self or soul. They are just functions of the physical body, such as *Thoughts*, *Perception*, *Emotion*, *Will*, and *Discriminative Intelligence*. The Soul is a separate and underlying entity from all these functions. It does not reside in any specific part of the body, but fills the entire body. The Soul is present in every living thing, not just humans, but also animals and plants.

Any living being, whether stationary or mobile, originates from the combination of body and Soul.

The soul is the essence of the Supreme Soul(*Paramatma*) who is the Creator of the infinite universe. The soul is a part of God who is the creator of the infinite universe. He is omnipresent in his nirgun-formless and sagun-sakar form. God resides in the heart of all beings and creatures. God appears in His physical form from time to time under the influence of devotion or love. Man is only a traveler and this traveler keeps traveling according to the results of his karma.

It is in a human being that we have certain privileges which we must use to uplift the soul and positively influence the life journey.

"How can we make this journey auspicious and happy while living in worldly life?", you will be able to know this in next chapter.

A worldly life can be a way to cleanse the soul. This requires eliminating the mind's attachments to self, wealth, power, and body.

God only gives humans the opportunity to perform karma or actions in this life. In other lives, they only face the consequences of their actions or karma.

Just imagine, if you do not make good use of human life, then after suffering karma in 840,0000 births, you will only get human life again.

Through good deeds and self-knowledge, in this human body, we can toil for the liberation of the soul or for salvation or moksha, which is a concept of ultimate freedom and liberation from the cycle of death and rebirth, also known as samsar. You can easily understand this self-knowledge after getting information about karma-yoga, sadhana or consciousness-gunas(quality of nature).

Karma, sadhana or conscious qualities help you in conquering the four subtle gatekeepers which are mind,   Satisfaction, discretion and Satsang

1. Mind

The meaning of mind may be different for different people, but mind is usually said to be the power that helps us think, perceive, experience and live life. The mind is the king of the body, which rules. But the mind has a habit of wandering. But through karma-yoga and sadhana you control the mind and save yourself from bad karmas or sins.

The indian vedic scriptures mention three kinds of sins:

1. *Physical* i.e., sin done by action;

2. *Verbal* i.e., sin done by speech;

3. *Mental* i.e., sin done by thought.

But for all these types of sin, the mind is involved; because there can be no deliberate act without the mind being there.

If the mind is not carefully guarded, desire will take its place in the senses, take possession of our thoughts, pollute our intellect and ultimately ruin us. So the battle must be fought with will at the door, when it seeks entry into our thoughts.

2. Satisfaction

Contentment means satisfying and calming your mind, body, and soul. Contentment frees us from sorrow and worries. To find contentment, we must love ourselves, our family, our friends, our work. We should be thankful for every little thing and enjoy our present life while moving towards our goals. A contented person always remains happy and lives in constant bliss.

Pleasures that arise from sensory contact are actually the source of unhappiness (though they appear to be pleasurable to worldly minds). They have a beginning and an end (they come and go). That is why the wise man does not indulge in them.

3. Discretion

Discretion means the correct use of your intellect or proper use of one's intelligence.

Man should awaken his conscience by knowledge. Those who do deeds with discretion and thought, their results are also good. It is wisdom that teaches us to distinguish between the superior and the best, between truth and falsehood, between the eternal and the immortal, between the soul and the matter. Discretion helps us to experience our soul, set the goal of our life, and accept the fruits of our actions. Man should make his future bright through thought and wisdom. In the context of the Bhagavad Gita, it is knowledge and wisdom that manifests in creating detachment in all actions.

4. Satsang

"Sat" means "permanent" and "Asat" means "one who leaves". Now we have to decide for ourselves how much time we have to stay with truth and how much time with untruth? The person who lives with truth is called a *satsangi*.

"*Sat*" is the soul and the divine which has always been there and which has existed since time immemorial.

In *Bhakti-Yoga*, *Sat* means God and *Sang* means the company of His loving devotees. Through satsang our mind becomes pure, peaceful and blissful, and we gain knowledge, devotion and experience of God. That is why a curious person should always make efforts for satsang.

We will discuss the complex subject of soul and bhakti yoga in coming chapters.

2

Spiritual Aspect of Yoga

1. What is the meaning of Yoga?

2. Are yoga and yoga asanas the same?

3. What is the yoga definition in modern life?

4. Is yoga related only to physical health?

5. What is the relation of yoga with spirituality?

Yoga is a Sanskrit word that means to connect or unite.

With whom do we connect?

*"**With the supreme reality.**"*

Who connects?

*"**The inner self.**"*

There are different mediums of yoga. Like asana, pranayama and meditation. All these help in connecting the soul(*atma*) with the Supreme Soul(*paramatma*) i.e. divine. Yoga not only balances physical health but also mental health.

Yoga's diverse forms across the globe today are all India's legacy. Our Vedas (sacred old Hindu texts) have the earliest mention of yoga, dating back thousands of years. Maharishi Patanjali's greatest achievement was integrating yoga into India's daily life.

Because yoga takes you from the worldly things towards the inner soul, that is why yoga is related to the soul, meditation and spiritual practice.

By following the path of Yoga, man can attain the five best qualities – strength, intelligence, courage and good character. Through yoga, we can significantly increase our efficiency and working capacity. Yoga keeps our mental health balanced, as a result of which it helps in getting rid of many diseases caused by today's modern lifestyle and that is why today mankind all over the world has understood its importance.

Yoga itself is a disciplined subject and it removes negativity from our body and mind. It develops and increase the healing power of our body. Through yoga you can control your life-giving breath and this practice is called **Pranayama.** *Prana* means vital air which travels through the nerves to every part of the body while inhaling and exhaling and keeps the body alive by giving it life. By practicing this, you keep the Prana-vayu(vital air) balanced in the body, which keeps your body healthy. There are many types of pranayam which our sages have told us from time to time.

Yoga asanas (physical postures) have an important relationship with meditation and *sadhana*. In *Siddhasana posture* You can awaken the powerful energy channels of your body called "Kundalini Awakening". Kundalini means a type of power which is wrapped in a coil in the lower part of the human spine. When this power is awakened, it provides many types of spiritual, mental and physical benefits to the person. To awaken the Kundalini, Kundalini Yoga is practiced, in which various pranayam, asanas, mudras, *bandhas*, meditation and mantras are used. This is such a complex subject of meditation and sadhana that it is impossible to explain it in one book.

Ayurveda has described yoga as a very important means of keeping the body healthy. Those who practice yoga in a disciplined manner can directly see the nature of their own soul.

There are eight important parts of yoga. Which has been named **Ashtanga Yoga.** Ashtanga Yoga is explained by Maharishi Patanjali in his book Yoga Sutra. The practice of Ashtanga Yoga leads to purification of body, mind, soul, health, peace and happiness. Asana (Physical Yoga) which is popular nowadays is just one of the types of Ashtanga yoga.

When you read the definition of all types of Ashtanga Yoga, then you will get to know why Yoga has so much importance in spirituality.

The eight limbs of Ashtanga Yoga are as follows.

1. Yam

Yam is a set of five rules, these are non-violence, truth, non-stealing, celibacy and non-greediness. By following the rules of Yama, man can increase his moral values. Yama teaches the art of living a practical life in accordance with Dharma.

2. Niyam

This is also a set of five rules, defecation, contentment, penance, self-study and devotion to God. It teaches the art of being disciplined in life and illuminates man's character.

3. Asanas(Posture)

These are different types of asanas to keep the body stable and happy. Asana teaches the art of keeping the body healthy. Asanas are a group of beneficial body postures as a result of which we can live a successful, happy and long life.

4. Pranayama

The one who teaches to give a new dimension or way to control breath or vital air.

It teaches the art of inhaling and exhaling so that every part of your body can get an adequate amount of vital air and your body always remains healthy.

5. Withdrawal(Pratyahara)

This is the practice of removing the senses from external objects and turning them inward. The art of controlling the senses of the body can be learned by the rules of Pratyahara. It helps in mental development.

6. Perception

It is the practice of putting the mind on one subject. It is also practiced as meditation or sadhana. It helps to concentrate the mind in the body part and to hold subtle content in the heart. By practicing perception one can reach the meditative state. Or rather, as a result of holding, man attains the meditative state.

7. Meditation

This is an exercise in concentrating the mind on the subject. Meditation helps us to achieve our goal in life easily. Through meditation we can attain knowledge of the soul.

8. Samadhi

It is a state of absorbing the mind into the subject. Attaining supreme bliss is possible through Samadhi. Samadhi, 'systematic form of meditation' is the next step. And do not make the mistake of thinking that Samadhi is only for saints and yogis. There is no need for you to abandon the household life.

You will also learn about this topic further in the book. By now you must have known that yoga teaches us the art of living in a positive way.

3

Gunas(Properties) of Nature

1. What is the importance of the three gunas – Sattva, Rajas and Tamas?
2. What is the relation of these three qualities to spirituality?
3. Can we see and experience these three qualities?
4. How can these three qualities be controlled?

The entire universe and the variables and immovable subjects and objects living in it always keep moving due to the change of three qualities or by the change of some desire. These three gunas are *tamas* (darkness & chaos), *rajas* (activity & passion), and *sattva* (beingness & harmony).

Sattva, Rajas and Tamas are the three qualities of nature, which affect our mind, body and soul. These qualities determine our personality, thoughts, feelings, actions and devotion.

Acharya Vinoba Bhave writes in one of his books that the person who can control his own senses can also rule this world of illusion. Now all of you readers must be a little surprised that I have just read about soul and yoga and after this why do we give so much importance to senses?

The senses are said to be larger than the body; but the mind is greater than the senses; wisdom is greater than the mind; and that which is greater than the wisdom and intellect is the *soul*.

The soul is complete and pure in itself. Due to these gunas the body is unable to see the soul. Due to these gunas, there is continuous origin and change of this mysterious universe and the variable and immovable beings and objects living in it. No subject matter can remain without being influenced by these gunas.

The important thing here is that these three gunas are necessary to fully enjoy family life and spiritual life. But when to adopt which qualities and when to awaken is a very difficult and complex task for humans. But these three qualities can be balanced and controlled. First of all let us try to know these three gunas.

These three qualities are present everywhere in every variable and invariable object.

Your body parts, senses, mind, brain and heart and not only this, your diet and even your activities have these three gunas. These gunas are controlled by you only but due to your ignorance you are not aware of it. These qualities determine the actions of your present life and future life.

Gunas also play a vital role in your karma(action). You will understand about karma in the next chapter.

Now only it is important to know these three gunas and balance them as much as possible. Tamasic guna affects humans negatively, hence we should always move from tamasic guna to sattva guna.

1. Tamas Gunas

First of all let us understand about the Tamasic gunas. And also know how the Tamas gunas can be taken to the rajas gunas. In today's modern lifestyle, it is very easy and simple to recognize the tamas gunas. Tamas guna represents ignorance, laziness, despair, indecisiveness, and destruction.

When do tamas guna affect you or when do you become tamasic? When tamasic qualities dominate our body, many distortions or negative behaviors affect us.

Consider these as side effects like,

- ❖ Laziness.
- ❖ Sleeping late at midnight.
- ❖ Sleeping till late in the morning.
- ❖ Drinking alcohol.
- ❖ Having negative thoughts.
- ❖ Causing unnecessary trouble to another human being.
- ❖ Consuming non-vegetarian food.

- ❖ Not keeping the body clean.

- ❖ And to spend your precious life as an indulgent person, without any charity-having done for good deeds.

- ❖ Thinking of harm to someone in one's mind.

- ❖ People with tamas guna do immoral and unrighteous actions to ruin their lives.

These distortions are just indicative points that can be used to identify many other tamasic states.

Balance of Tamas Gunas

How to balance tamas gunas? Because you have known the importance of yoga. And in my opinion, through yoga also you can balance or neutralize the tamas gunas.

For example, by practicing yoga postures regularly, you can cure disorders like laziness or in other words, social disorders. After daily practice of yoga asanas you will see yourself that your tamasic gunas are getting balanced and gradually becoming inactive.

As I wrote, the entire universe is continuously functioning due to the change of these three gunas. Therefore, it cannot be the case that scholars have only one guna everywhere, satvik and rajas gunas will also always be there in some percentage. You can say that the whole game is about controlling this percentage. And I believe where all these gunas will become zero percent, you assume that there is liberation, salvation and that nature of soul is the ultimate goal of humans.

I can understand. These things are quite complicated at this time. But in the coming chapters you will be able to get more information about them.

2. Rajas Gunas

It is a bit difficult to understand spiritual matters. Because you have to understand this only with deep inner feelings and faith. You should understand it in such a way that not only in the world but in the universe, every moving object is always engaged in some activity or the other. And this process continues due to Rajas Gunas. And you must have understood that if there is no kriya(work) then it is affected by Tamas Gunas. You will be surprised that this universe itself is born due to a desire and rajas gunas. Nowadays even scientists have started believing that spiritual matters exist.

Let's discuss an interesting theory, if you think about how the universe was created, you will find that it is the same from both a scientific and spiritual point of view.

Where science says that the universe was created due to Big-Bang-Theory. Indian Spiritual theories also say that the first sound which we call "Om" in our Vedas originated from this Universe due to which the whole Universe was born. All these changes happen due to a change in the three guna in both the above theories. When the Big Bang was still or it had no sound, it was tamas guna, and when sound transfer took place, rajo guna action and activities took place. Because of these actions a lot of positive and negative changes happened. When these changes are negative, we see events like earthquakes, volcanoes, and climate changes. And when this change is positive, we can see greenery in nature and there is joy among habitants.

Because we are also a part of the universe, rajas gunas also affect us in positive and negative ways.

Rajas guna represents activity, enthusiasm, craving, aggression, and growth.

People with rajas guna are obsessive, selfish, restless, impatient and Rajasic.

You must have understood this here that if no action is taking place then the subject and object are affected by tattva or tamas guna.

The activities carried out by rajas guna accumulate the karma of a human being or in other words, it makes a human being do the karma. And this is also one of the definitions of karma.

You have now come to know that the soul, the "I" that is within you, keeps an account of all those deeds.

If you don't pause and think a little, then this rajas guna can affect you very seriously. People with rajasic qualities compete and struggle to achieve their goals. Because its tendency is to change all the time. If a little restraint or attention is lost then there is every possibility of disaster happening.

You can try to identify when rajas guna can affect you through the following feelings.

1. When someone has a desire to do everything as quickly as possible.

2. When someone has a strong desire to accomplish political or spiritual goals quickly.

3. When innumerable thoughts come to the mind and those thoughts cause sorrow or pleasure to the body and mind in some way or the other.

Now it depends on you how you will take Rajas guna in a positive direction?

If you take Rajas guna in a positive direction then you will be happy and will achieve fame in the society. On the other hand, if rajas guna is taken in a negative and egoistic direction, then in the end one will have to be ready to suffer the consequences like Ravana.

Today man has been able to know about many secrets of nature due to positive rajas guna. By trying not to balance the rajas guna , today the entire human race is fighting many problems on a war footing due to the crime of tampering with nature. Even scientists have accepted that if we do not improve then there is a 100 percent possibility that we, the human race, which is the best among living beings, will disappear from the universe.

Let us discuss how to make Rajas guna useful for oneself. First of all, try to control your physical and mental energy. This life is very simple, you accept it.

And if you want to run this life by behaving like a wrestler then stop it immediately.

I am giving such an example because when rajas guna is prevalent in your body and mind, a large amount of energy is emitted. To utilize this energy positively is to balance rajas guna.

Whenever you feel that you need immediate results of any work then accept that rajas guna is dominating you. And now you have to adopt a balancing process. You can ease this by giving some pause to your physical and mental activities. Why this, because due to the influence of rajas guna, you can lose your physical and mental balance and if you do not maintain the balance, then you can turn from sattva guna state to tamas guna and then there are fair chances that you perform negative actions.

When Rajas guna dominates, a person's body and mind do not remain stable, he keeps changing his decisions very quickly. Not only this, sometimes he also loses self-confidence.

Well, in this worldly and practical life. All the programs are going on due to Rajas guna only. But due to the lack of balance of Rajas guna many tasks also get spoiled. That is why by balancing rajas guna, you can bring very important positive changes for yourself and mankind.

For now, you can do this when rajas guna is telling the body or mind to act. You can divide actions into many small tasks. This will reduce its effect. And you will find it easier to make decisions and this situation takes you in the direction of virtuous qualities.

Shri Vinoba Bhave has tried to explain this by giving an example in one of his books.

"He said that when the rain drops fall on the top of the mountain, the mountain sends them into all its small cracks, due to which the intensity of the rain reduces and as the water droplets decrease, they also become invisible (extinct)."

This is an indicative example which you can remember and as it will help in taking further decisions.

3. Sattva Guna

This is the only quality in social and practical life which is present everywhere in all subjects. But we deliberately refuse to recognize the Sattva quality under the influence of Tamas and Rajas guna.

Sattva Guna represents purity, knowledge, peace, love and joy. People with sattva qualities are kind, selfless, pure, intelligent and virtuous. They have a feeling of reverence, devotion and dedication towards God. They do spiritual practices to experience their soul(atma).

All objects and behavior around us are also divided into the three gunas and we have read this before.

Here is how you can identify the virtue of goodness.

If you talk about diet, you must have heard that non-vegetarian food is considered a tamasic food, for which there are many scientific facts and evidence which proves this. What changes can occur in your body by eating tamasic food, the tendencies of tamasic qualities become dominant after eating it, the same results have also emerged from scientific facts that eating non-vegetarian food causes more work to the digestive system of the body. Due to which your mind also gets filled with laziness. Sometimes even human behavior becomes aggressive. On the other hand, if you eat vegetarian or satvik food, your body easily saves this food in a short time and converts it into energy. And then there is a feeling of new freshness coming into your body.

Identifying sattva is very simple. If you remove the tamas guna and rajas guna mentioned above from your physical and mental body through remedies which I mentioned above, then what remains is called sattva guna.

This topic will also seem a bit complicated to you right now, but once you read the answer further about Karma and recognize the importance of Karma, then this chapter and its adoption will seem simple and useful.

Because gunas of nature are related to actions. These gunas transform your actions into good deeds(karma) or sinful deeds(karma). You will be able to understand karma in detail in the upcoming chapter.

4
Karma (Deeds)

1. What is the definition of karma?

2. What is the spiritual and practical importance of karma?

3. What is the social importance of karma?

4. What is meant by good karma and bad karma?

5. Karma-Yoga, why is karma called yoga in this?

6. Who is a Karma-Yogi?

7. What is the relation of karma to the Soul?

8. Why should we not worry about the results of our actions?

9. What is the relation between the karma(deeds) of previous birth and the present and future?

10. Why did Lord Krishna give so much importance to karma in the Greatest Holy Book Shrimad Bhagvad Gita?

11.Can a man give up the fruits of his actions?

The totality of our thoughts, feelings and actions is called **Karma(Deeds)**. Man is bound by his karma, and develops himself according to his actions, this process continues until death and the next life.

Our life is created and controlled by karma. We get the fruits of our actions(deeds), whether they are good or bad. Our birth, death, happiness, sorrow, heaven, hell and salvation all depend on our karma. Karma is a complex subject that is not easy to understand by relating it to every person, but my readers should be rest assured, I will do my work, whatever the result.

You must be wondering why I told the essence of Gita, that "*keep doing your work and don't worry about the results*".

Shri Krishna might have said this statement because he would know that the worldly man would be sad and disappointed if his wish is not fulfilled, God cannot see his own part "Jivatma(living soul)" sad. Here the essence is, make use of the worldly things, but do not attach importance with them, nor accept your own ego of possession over them.

Now we will discuss karma by connecting it with spirituality. Our sages and wise men have given principles to perform the karma in the right way so that when the action is taking place, then with the help of these principles, one can decide to choose the right path of action and that action is transformed into good karma.

Only through good Karma can a man live a happy and joyful life.

It is difficult to stop actions. No one can stop karma, the entire universe is functioning due to karma and karma has become a continuously occurring activity. You can be a subject of this action or even consider yourself the doer of actions.

Here karma is not only a physical action but also a mental action. For example, when you are sitting in a conscious state or traveling, at that time also your mind is controlling your actions. It is not possible that you are not a part of the karmic process. This is possible only when you have gone into eternal sleep or complete trance(*Samadhi*). You will be able to read about Samadhi in detail in the next chapter.

Now let us try to know and adopt how through the principles of karma we can increase our good deeds and reduce the consequences of sinful deeds.

Believe it or not, nothing happens in the universe and in your life without a reason and the presence of a will or desire. Whatever this desire comes from your outer body, it first comes into your inner self and then from the inner body to your brain. After that an order passes to your mind to take actions. When your mind is thinking about the decision, this is where you get full time to re-think, understand and make right decisions. And with the same conscience you can now give orders to the parts of your body. This process happens all the time in your body.

But why does it become so difficult to make decisions? Because of two desires, two thoughts are giving two decisions, one positive and the other negative. When any desire comes to your mind, you have to work according to *Dharma*(righteous duty).

The Gita also distinguishes between different types of *dharma*(duty), some are as follows:

Self-Duty(Savdharma): One's own personal duty, which is based on his innate qualities, abilities, and inclinations.

Life Stage Duty(Ashrama-Dharma):
Ashrama-Dharma is based on the four stages of human life,

    1. *Brahmacharya* (Student),
    2. *Grihastha* (Householder),
    3. *Vanaprastha* (Retired),
    4. And *sannyasa* (Renunciation).

Ashrama-dharma is the righteous duties(dharma) that guides the spiritual growth and development of a person, and prescribes different rules and practices for different stages of life.

Let us take a simple example from personal life, there is a diabetic patient and you present him something sweet to consume like *Rasgulla(Indian sweet)*.

We all know that not only us but even a diabetic patient's mouth will fill with water. One of his desires will order him to eat and the other will tell him not to do so. Now here is the patient's self responsibility, which is his own *Svadharma* and he has to consider what is the patient's dharma towards his body. And this decision will determine the outcome of the action. If the patient takes the decision according to his own *svadharma* and the *svadharma* of the patient, then you have done a good deed, the result of your action will be good. And if you do not follow your svadharma, the result of karma can also be bad.

This was a very simple example. But then complexity arises when we have to follow dharmas in our practical and social life.

Now how should we work for ourselves and the society? Which principles and rules should we follow with our actions? To take this topic of karma further, we have to pause and understand the topic of *shamajik dharma(Social Obligations)*, when the righteous *dharma* is practiced in society, it leads to *Shamajik Dharma*

Here you should not connect this *dharma* with any religious belief. If you do this then this *dharma* which we want to define through spirituality will move towards one's faith or *Bhakti(Devotion)*. We will also discuss this topic of *Bhakti* in the next chapter.

Now let us again connect with *dharma* and karma. In this universe, the movable and immovable objects and subjects are connected to some gunas and they keep working according to that nature. Today science is also trying to understand this thing which we call natural. Even science says it by quoting the word *natural* for all unknown.

But in spirituality, we connect the nature traits of every living being with its definite karma and we consider this tendency as its *svadharma*. The meaning of *svadharma* is those rules which are related to ourselves, which we have to follow, which is our nature.

Let us try to understand this topic by simplifying it a bit and using some spiritual examples.

The duty of the Sun God in the universe is to provide continuous light to the whole universe and to all living and nonliving things in the universe. And *Suryadev*(Sun God) follows his *svadharma*. Suryadev always keeps doing this action and work. And this positive karma keeps all the creatures, plants and animals of the universe alive. That is why Sun God becomes worshipable for us. And because of this, we consider all the rays of light, whether it is a temple lamp, a house light or any other light that is not in use, as a part of the Sun God.

Let us take another example, if we think about the nature of a creature like a tiger, its nature is carnivorous. However, his *svadharma* says that he can use other living beings as food and he kills living beings according to his own *svaDharma*. This cannot be his misdeed.

Now let us try to understand this through a more practical example. When a doctor (surgeon) dissects a body part of a sick patient and due to some reason he dies. Then we can say that there is no bad effect of karma on the doctor, because socially and practically he was following his *svadharma*.

Let us take another example from the family of a householder. Every householder should work hard to nurture his family.

But when that work is done with the intention of cheating, dishonesty or causing harm to others, then that work turns into bad deeds or sin.

Some of my dear readers may say, "Many times a person dies of hunger in this world without any dishonesty. Isn't it the definition of right action for the stomach that it can indulge in dishonesty to satisfy the hunger of the stomach?" "

We can understand that hunger can force a person to commit many sinful acts, but still we cannot call it a good deed, because that social misdeed can affect you too somewhere and it is against social duty(*samajik dharma*). Otherwise, living in a jungle, where there are no rules and regulations, and living in a worldly and social environment will be the same. Therefore, we will call it a sinful act.

There is a very thin line between good karma and bad karma. While doing good karma in this social and practical life, we may face many problems. We may have to give up a lot, we may have to face a lot of tests and when we move forward in that test with patience, thoughtfulness, sacrifice and suffering, it becomes the result of our good karma and here I would like to tell you, these good karma will give you self-confidence, satisfaction. It makes your atma happy and this is where the karma gets connected with the atma and the atma which is separate from your body takes those karmas and takes you back to some blissful world.

Therefore, I would suggest that you do your work while thinking about your own *dharma*, ashrama dharma and social *dharma* .

For my beloved readers, I would like to share the definition of types of dharmas that can be understood as one's duty, role, or purpose in life. According to the Gita, dharma is not a fixed or rigid concept, but rather a dynamic and relative one, depending on one's nature, situation, and stage of life. The Gita teaches that one should follow one's svadharma, even if it is imperfect, rather than imitating someone else's dharma, which may be more virtuous but unsuitable for one's personality and circumstances. By doing so, one can attain peace, happiness, and liberation from the cycle of birth and death.

The Gita also explains that dharma is not a rigid or dogmatic law, but a flexible and rational principle that can be adjusted according to time, place, and circumstance. For example, Krishna tells Arjuna that in the present situation of war, his dharma as a kshatriya is to fight for justice and protect the righteous, even if it means killing his relatives and teachers, who have become corrupted and adharmic. Krishna also tells Arjuna that he can transcend the ordinary dharma of karma (action and reaction) by performing his actions as a sacrifice to God, without attachment to the results. By doing so, he can achieve the supreme dharma of bhakti (devotion), which is the ultimate goal of all dharmas.

Therefore, the Gita teaches that dharma is not a static or absolute concept, but a dynamic and relative one, that depends on one's nature, situation, and goal.

Let us know a little more about the results of karma, as we had read in the beginning that one has to keep doing the karma but not worry about the results. Today's youth, after setting goals in life, are always worried about their results. If we have this much faith in our goal, then we should not worry about it. We should give our full contribution in doing the present work. But it is not so, today we keep thinking that what will happen if there is failure in achieving the goal, many worldly problems may arise. By desiring results, your physical and mental energy keeps getting wasted.

If you consider yourself to be just a means and do not worry about the result of the goal, then negative thoughts will not come in your mind and you will focus only on working hard, by doing this the goal will be achieved and its pride and ego will not come.

And if you do not get it, then you will not feel inferior to think that you have not made your full contribution but learned a lot which you can be ready to work hard to improve again. As a result, you can also become a role model for others.

If you have understood even a little about karma till now, then believe me, you are able to use some part of Shrimad Bhagvad Gita in your life.

As you have understood, no one can run away from karma, but if you act according to the principles of karma then you will be called a karmayogi. A karma-yogi always keeps earning virtue. Because for a karma-yogi, any work mentioned in svadharma and social dharma is not just a work but for him it becomes like a penance, a worship, a worship. In the end, the result of worship is received in the form of *Prasad(holy blessing)*, but by following svadharma, the karma-yogi continues to receive its *Prasad* in the form of satisfaction and joy at every moment.

Shri Krishna has said in the Gita that one who performs his duty without expecting the fruits of actions is both a sannyasin(*a Hindu religious mendicant)* and a karma yogi. Let us look at another aspect of karma, every person in life chooses the work which he likes, otherwise he does not want to do the work, but this is also called selfishness. If you are a karma-yogi and are a part of this universe, you have to fulfill your responsibilities otherwise negative thoughts will keep troubling you.

We should consider every day as a new routine and not get tired. A karma-yogi should keep trying to complete every task with joy. And then there is no need to worry about the results of your actions.

In the Gita, Shri Krishna told Arjuna, "*O Arjuna, there is neither any duty for Me in the three worlds, nor is there anything attainable or unattainable for Me; Yet I continue to work.*".

That is the reason, God has incarnated many times and taught us the way to follow the path of action. Lord Shri Krishna himself came as a cowherd and served the animals, he himself became the charioteer of Arjun and served the horses of Arjun's chariot and the same Lord became the king of Dwarka and served the people.

We can say that you keep working. And have faith in God and renounce the desire of outcome or fruit. By doing this you gradually move inward and is another step to connecting with the soul(atma).

When you do not desire the results of your actions, you become a recluse in household life. Your mind becomes single-minded and engages in some sort of meditation(*dhayan*). We will understand and discuss this meditation in the next chapter.

Like I said, all these chapters are connected to each other as a link, but the goal of all is the same.

5
Meditation

1. Can we connect with the soul (atma) through meditation and spiritual practice?

2. After all, how can one concentrate whereas the human mind is of such a fickle nature?

3. Can the path of meditation(dhyan and sadhana) and its practice be followed only by a sannyasi?

4. Can't everyone practice this? If yes, then what benefit will an average person, student and youth get from it in their daily routine?

Let us once again reiterate the basic goal of spirituality. The ultimate goal of spirituality is to achieve supreme happiness, supreme bliss, peace, salvation, liberation and union of the soul(self and *jivatma)* with God(*paramatma*). I am giving different names to all these here, but all these are different names of the same feeling.

For example, there may be many different routes to the top of a mountain. Similarly, you can also achieve the ultimate goal through yoga, self-knowledge, action, meditation, sadhana and devotion. The word devotion(*bhakti*) has been introduced here which can raise different types of questions in your mind. But rest assured, we will try to understand devotion also in the next chapter.

Now we will try to understand meditation in a simple way.

Meditation means concentration or pervading thought. Meditation makes the mind calm and healthy, increases concentration and memory power, reduces stress and anxiety, gives a feeling of confidence and self-realization.

The process of meditation includes worship, yoga, concentration, chanting, fasting, penance etc. Through meditation, a person purifies, calms and concentrates his mind, and experiences unity with his *Paramatma*(eternal soul).

Dhayan and *Sadhana* is a spiritual method that helps in bringing the mind to a calm state which keeps you mentally and physically healthy, and also makes your lifestyle and daily routine happy. Now the western countries have given the name of Dhayan to meditation, the meaning of which has also been taken as meditek or medicare.

This shows that even the world has understood that the *dhayan* and *sadhana* kriya and its methods given by the sages of India, are very important for maintaining complete health.

Now if we want to understand Meditation then you can say that it is an attempt to connect the atma(soul) with Paramatma(eternal soul or God). For *sadhana* one should practice it regularly and follow the guidance of one's guru, if you are lucky to get a true one. In India, there are different forms of sadhana of saints, such as knowledge, karma, yoga and *bhakti*.

Nirguna Bhakti(formless devotion) has an important place in the sadhana of saints, in which they consider God to be devoid of name, form, virtue and lila. The spiritual practice of saints includes elements like devotion, satsang, Guru, chanting the name, renunciation, charity, self-reconciliation etc. The purpose of the sadhana of saints is to purify, calm and concentrate your mind, and to know the nature of your atma. By worshiping , the saints, they free themselves from the illusions and sorrows of the world, and experience the love and joy of God.

There are many negative notions about meditation spread around us like someone may say that if you do not have any work then you should meditate, do sadhana. Some other people will say that you should give up the earthly life and take *sannyasa* and then do meditation and sadhana. And you will hear and see other similar things and concepts in front of you and around you.

But you should know this, all this is due to ignorance. We all should try to share the knowledge we have received. Even if it is a little, it should continue to circulate around us through some medium or the other, so that negative thinking can be transformed into positive thinking to some extent.

As you start practicing meditation in your life, you will experience many positive results. Like,

- ❖ Your enjoyment of life will increase.
- ❖ Your thoughts and conversations will become clearer.
- ❖ You will feel complete satisfaction.
- ❖ You will find it easier to take the most difficult decisions of life.
- ❖ Not only mental benefits but you also get physical benefits from meditation and sadhana.

These are just some experiences, but there are many more experiences associated with every person which you cannot write in words. As we have learned in yoga, today's lifestyle has given rise to many diseases which science and medical science have named as mental stress, hypertension, stress or lifestyle-related diseases or diseases of the muscular system. You must have heard about all these complaints from your relatives and friends around you.

Meditation can be the best remedy for these types of lifestyle diseases. By meditating, the flow of *pranavayu(vital air)* becomes easier and it reaches every part of the body and controls the energy associated with the body parts. It results in a slight pause in your mental and physical activity and these effects free you from the diseases caused by your lifestyle. You will also find that meditation helps you bring changes in your behavior such as controlling anger, controlling appetite, even sleep.

You have seen the benefits of meditation but now you might be wondering how to do it?

First of all let us try to understand how to meditate. The best part is that meditation is a very simple process. But when it gradually takes the form of sadhana, it becomes a little complicated. Nowadays many wise meditation practioner have popularized this in many versatile ways to make it easier for the individual and this is good too. Whatever may be the way and the method, the goal, as I said, is the same.

Meditation is an introverted method. It takes you from the material world to the inner soul of the body and only when you are introverted, you get a chance to interview your atma(soul) and this is the link that connects meditation to the atma(soul).

The definition of meditation is not sitting quietly, because your restless mind is always working. Meditation makes you try to keep your mind focused on a given goal by removing it from external thoughts.

This goal can be anything, a sound, a picture, a mantra or the chanting of a name. One of the reasons for this is that this meditation method is not the same for everyone where everyone can be made to sit and understand in the same way.

The mind of every person and his personal character, is busy searching for answers to the questions which are constantly arising in his mind. Therefore, keeping in mind the behavior and current state of each person, it is advisable for some to concentrate on the *sound*, for some to *chant the name(naam-japa)*, for some to concentrate on the movement of breathing and for some to concentrate on the picture. And this is called the first stage of meditation.

We already know that meditation has also been a form of yoga. That means you use *Sukhasana*, *Padmasana*, *Pranayam-Mudra* for meditation. It is proved here that meditation also helps you in connecting your soul(*atma*) and attaining that ultimate happiness and bliss.

You can meditate by sitting in any simple yoga posture or if you feel healthy, try in *padmasana* posture.

In the beginning, meditating is a little difficult. Because it is natural that many external and internal activities bother you and your mind. But you should also accept that the very function of meditation is to free you from all external and internal actions and thoughts and keep you practicing and focusing only on a given goal.

At this stage of spirituality topics, I can understand many of the questions arising in my readers mind. Somewhere you may find spirituality a little complicated to understand, but there is a valid reason for this too. I believe, earlier it was not such a difficult subject because somewhere the influence of *Gurukul* specialized spiritual education was all over India where meditation, sadhana, yoga and devotion were taught as academic subjects. Nowadays this is not the case in the curriculum of our schools. Perhaps this is the reason why our body, mind and brain find it very difficult to accept it.

But you should be happy that today the whole world is not only praising this unique knowledge discovered and popularized by our Indian sages and gurus.

Preparing to meditate

Before preparing for meditation, be sure to know that it is not a process of contemplation, nor is it a method of hypnotization. Meditation is so simple that you do not control any of the senses of the body, rather you as an observer feel the activities happening in the body. Before meditating, you need to understand some meditations prerequisites and rules. Like,

- ❖ First of all, you need to know how to bring the body to a state of relaxation
- ❖ How to give a comfortable posture to the body
- ❖ How to let the *pranvayu*(vital air) flow in every part of your body without any interruption.

* How we can let the thoughts come and go without reacting to them physically or mentally.

* How to get rid of the turmoil and tingling sensation in the body?

Method of meditation and its benefits

Your goal, interest and practice determine the method of meditation. Meditation has different types and methods in many religions and traditions, such as Buddhist meditation, Jain meditation, etc.

To start with, you can choose a quiet and clean place for meditation, where you will not have any interruptions. Before meditating, your body should be healthy. If you are getting treatment for any disease which makes you a little uncomfortable, then you should wait for some time for the body to become free from the disease. Also before meditating, make your body and mind are pure and sacred. You can take a bath, brush your teeth, correct your posture, dress your body in comfortable clothes, take a few deep breaths to calm your mind. Also try to do warm up exercises like stretching or simple yoga asanas.

Sitting in a comfortable position

As mentioned above, you can adopt any comfortable posture as per your body capacity. Healthy people can also use *Padmasana*. Sitting in *Sukhasana* is also beneficial for meditation. Not only that, a person can also practice meditation by sitting in any comfortable chair. But make sure your spine should be straight and body lose while sitting.

Selection of time

You can meditate at any time when you feel calm and fresh. But dawn, early morning time or dusk, sunset is considered good for meditation.

Selection of fine targets

While meditating, keep your breathing normal, keep your eyes closed, focus on your goal, calm your thoughts, control your emotions, keep your body comfortable.

You can practice meditation using any symbol, picture or listening to an echo sound.

Some examples of symbolic-goals are as follows-

- ❖ Seeing your favorite Gods and Goddesses through pictures.
- ❖ Pronouncing the sound of "ॐ" (Om) from the heart.
- ❖ Chanting Gayatri Mantra in mind.
- ❖ Feeling of breathing coming in and out of the nostril.

Sitting & Time Limit

While meditating,
- keep your breathing normal,
- keep your eyes closed,
- focus on your goal,
- calm your thoughts,
- control your emotions,
- keep your body comfortable.

Meditation time depends on your purpose, interest and practice. You can meditate for 5 to 10 minutes in the beginning, and gradually increase it. You can meditate daily or thrice in a week, but regularity and devotion are essential. I would recommend making meditation your lifestyle and doing it as a daily routine. As this will become a part of your daily routine, there is nothing to follow the schedule, so be patient, do not rush.

How to check the result of meditation

Meditation does not curb your thinking and speaking but rather matures your thinking and speaking power. You will gradually see that there is a positive change in your behavior towards every person and also there is a change in the reaction of that person too.

This meditation(*Dhayan*) only takes the form of *Sadhana* and *Samadhi* with continuous practice and then you come face to face with the ultimate goal which every human being practices to achieve. But do remember this is a practice and you should not covet the results. This practice is similar to the way the *ocean is churned*(*sagar-mantan*), apart from the target of nectar-pot(*amrit-kalash*), many beneficial things emerge from the churning. Similarly, there is a lot to be found in the path of meditation, sadhana, yoga and devotion which makes our life joyful.

Finally, here are few more benefits of meditation -

- Meditation improves concentration and memory, which leads to success in your studies, work and life.

- Meditation makes your mind calm and happy, thereby relieving you from anxiety, fear, anger, apathy, stress and other mental problems.

- With meditation, your body becomes healthy and strong, which protects you from pain, fatigue, physical weakness and other physical problems.

- Meditating brightens and purifies your mind, allowing you to experience self-confidence, realization, joy, peace, love, compassion, kindness, forgiveness and other spiritual qualities.

6

Devotion as Spiritual Practice

1. What is the relation of devotion(*bhakti*) with spirituality?

2. Why is devotion so important in Hindu religion?

3. Should the path of devotion be started only at old age?

My dear readers, you may say that devotion is the domain of God believers, what does it have to do with meditation and spirituality? Or Is the talk of worship also becoming a part of spirituality?

It is true that if Yoga, Karma, Meditation and Sadhana are one side of the ocean then Devotion(Bhakti) is the other side. But as we now know that the goal is the same, the attainment of supreme happiness and bliss. Devotion and spirituality complement each other, and influence each other. Devotion increases the power of spirituality, and spirituality increases the depth of devotion. The ultimate goal of devotion and spirituality is the same, the realization of God. Both devotion and spirituality are feelings of love and dedication towards God or *Paramatma*.

In devotion, a person worships his favorite deity, chants his name, remembers his *lilas* and takes shelter of his blessings. In devotion, a person considers himself a servant of God, and lives his life according to his wishes. A devotee who has full faith and reverence in any deity, scripture, and five elements can also achieve the goal of that bliss. Devotion is not only the name of worship, but also of nivikalpa(without any alternative), selfless and unwavering love.

When you consider someone as an object of devotion and remember him in every breath, then you can always keep experiencing that ecstasy through devotion. That experience can never be written in words. The character of a true and devoted devotee(*bhakt*) is always like that of a small child who just wants to be with his mother. This is a devotional feeling of unwavering love.

The feeling of devotion can come in the form of any relation in the mind of the devotees. For example, Meerabai considered Krishna as her husband and lived in that blissful state by singing his praises day and night.

The same devotee Chaitanya Mahaprabhu, who merged himself in Radha(Krisha's beloved) and was always engrossed in devotion to Krishna and while leading a social life. Chaitanya Mahaprabhu was always engrossed in Krishna bhajans(devotion songs) and led a social life.

Not only this, the supreme devotee Hanuman had finally refused to go to *Bhagavatalok Vaikuntha* with Shri Rama himself to listen to the character and hymns of

Shri Rama. That's the reason, he wanted to live on earth and experience the ultimate bliss of devotion to God continuously.

Devotion also takes you within your inner self and provides true happiness and strength which you can never experience with material comforts. Devotion inspires you to serve humanity because after becoming a devotee you have understood that all living beings are experiencing happiness and sorrow through the same vital-air and soul(*atma*) which is also present within you. Devotion destroys your ego because you come to know that ultimate happiness is not outside but within you. Devotion brings generosity and high values in you and that helps you to experience social happiness. Devotion creates immense faith in you due to which you always have the ability to struggle with even the toughest situations. A true devotee becomes *a saint* when he sorrows in the sorrows of others; and remains happy in the happiness of others.

Some Great Saints of India

1. Chaitanya Mahaprabhu

To tell about Chaitanya Mahaprabhu in words is not an easy task, because his life and achievements are so vast and profound that it is impossible to cover them in a short essay. Still, I will try to tell you some key things about them.

Chaitanya Mahaprabhu was a 15th-century Hindu saint and spiritual leader who founded the Gaudiya Vaishnavism movement. He is considered an incarnation of Lord Krishna and Radha by his followers. Chaitanya Mahaprabhu (February 18, 1486-1534) is the ultimate propagator of Bhakti Yoga of Vaishnava religion and one of the major poets of the Bhakti period. He popularized the chanting of the Hare Krishna mantra and composed the Siksastakam, a prayer of eight verses in Sanskrit. He also taught the philosophy of Achintya Bheda Abheda, which means "inconceivable oneness and difference" between God and his energies.

He travelled extensively throughout India, spreading his teachings and performing ecstatic kirtans. He laid the foundation stone of the Gaudiya sect of Vaishnavas, gave birth to a new style of bhajan singing and in the days of political instability, strengthened the goodwill of Hindu-Muslim unity, taught to remove casteism, the feeling of high and low and re-established the extinct Vrindavan and spent the last part of his life there.

He was born in a village called Navadeep (Nadia) in West Bengal, which is now called Mayapur. He was born in the evening during the lunar eclipse in Leo ascendant. At that time, many people were going to bathe in Ganga chanting Hari naam(*chanting God Vishnu name*) with the desire of purification. Then the learned Brahmins, taking into account the planets in his horoscope and the omens present at that time, predicted that this child would preach Harinam throughout his life.

His name in childhood was Vishvambhar, but everyone called him Nimai because it is said that he was found under a Neem tree(Azadirachta indica). Because of his fair complexion, people also called him

Gaurang(*whose body color is golden*), Gaur Hari, Gaur Sundar etc. His father's name was Jagannath Mishra and mother's name was Shachi Devi.

Nimai has been prodigiously talented since childhood. At the same time, he was very simple, beautiful and emotional. Everyone was astonished to see the *lilas*(pastimes) performed by them. At a very young age, Nimai became proficient in justice and grammar. Nimai remained engrossed in the contemplation of God and started singing praises of Ram and Krishna. He spent the last 18 years of his life in Puri, where he died in 1534.

2. Mirabai

Mirabai's life and achievements are so vast and profound that again it is impossible to cover them in a short essay.

Merabai (1498–1547) was a Krishna devotee and poet of the sixteenth century. She was one of the most popular Bhakti saints of the Bhakti movement. His hymns dedicated to Lord Krishna are still very popular in North India and are sung with devotion.

Merabai was born in a royal family of Rajasthan. Merabai's father's name was Ratan Singh and she was the great-granddaughter of Jodhpur-founder Rao Jodha. His mother died in his childhood, Hence, she lived with her grandfather Rao Jodha ji. He also received his primary education by staying with his grandfather. Ravda ji was of very religious and liberal nature which had a complete impact on Mirabai's life. Merabai was a devotee of Krishna since childhood.

Merabai was married into the Sisodia royal family of Mewar. Her husband was Maharaja Bhojraj of Chittorgarh, who was the son of Maharana Sanga of Mewar. Her husband died shortly after marriage. After her husband's death, an attempt was made to commit *sati** with her, but Mirabai was not ready for it. The last rites of Mirabai's husband took place in Chittor in the absence of Mirabai. Even after the death of her husband, Mirabai Mata did not remove her makeup, because she considered Lord Krishan(Girdhar) as her husband.

Mirabai started spending her time doing Harikirtan(devotional songs) in the company of sages and saints. After her husband's death, her devotion increased day by day. She used to go to temples and dance in front of the idol of Krishna in front of the Krishna devotees present there. The royal family did not like Mirabai's dancing and singing in devotion to Krishna. He tried several times to kill Mirabai by poisoning her. She was fed up with this kind of behavior of her family members, so she went to Dwarka and Vrindavan. Wherever she went, people respected her. People loved and respected her like a goddess.

**Sati Pratha was a bad Hindu custom in which the widow of the dead man immolated herself willingly by sitting on his funeral pyre. The practice of Sati in ancient times was voluntary, but during the medieval period, it might have been forced on some widows. Later it is eradicated completely.*

3. Saint Tukaram

Tukaram (1598-1650) was a prominent saint and poet of the Varkari sect of Maharashtra. He was a great devotee of Lord Vitthal or Vithoba, who is considered to be an incarnation of Vishnu. He used to give the message of devotion and equality through his abhangas(*speeches*) and kirtans. In his abhangas he has expressed his life's adversities, joys, introspection and love for God. His abhangas are considered priceless gems of Marathi language.

Tukaram was born in a Kunbi family in Dehu village near Pune. His father's name was Bolhoba and mother's name was Kanakai. His father was a businessman and farmer. There was a tradition of worshiping vitthal in his family. His parents died in his childhood. He took over the family business along with his brother Santoba. He married twice. His first wife was Rakhumabai and second wife was Avalibai. He had three children.

Tukaram had to face many difficulties in his life. His first wife and one son died due to famine. His second wife had differences with him. His business also went into loss. He had difficulty maintaining his devotion amidst his social and family duties. He had to face criticism and ridicule even from the people of his own society. With the inspiration of his Guru Babaji Chaitanya, he handed over all his problems to God.

Tukaram spent most of his life chanting the name of God, writing hymns, kirtans and abhangas. He expressed his experiences, thoughts, feelings and teachings in his Abhangas. In his Abhangas, there is coordination of philosophies like Vedanta, Yoga, Bhakti, Knowledge, Karma, Bhagya, Nirguna, Saguna, Advaita, Dvaita, Vishishtadvaita etc. In his Abhangas he has depicted his intimate dialogue with God. They have called God as their friend, companion, beloved, husband, father, mother, guru, protector, refuge, master etc.

4. Ramakrishna Paramahamsa

Ramakrishna Paramahamsa, a 19th-century Hindu saint and the founder of the Ramakrishna Order of monks. He is regarded as the spiritual founder of the Ramakrishna Movement, which aims to spread his teachings of universal harmony and service to humanity. He was also the guru of Swami Vivekananda, one of the most influential spiritual leaders of modern India.

Ramakrishna was born in 1836 in Kamarpukur, a village in Bengal. He had a mystical temperament from a young age and was drawn to various forms of devotion and worship. He became a priest at the Dakshineswar Kali Temple in Kolkata, where he practiced different paths of Hinduism, such as Tantra, Vaishnavism, and Advaita Vedanta. He also had experiences of other religions, such as Islam and Christianity, and affirmed that all religions lead to the same God.

Ramakrishna had a profound influence on many people who came in contact with him, including scholars, artists, social reformers, and religious seekers. He attracted a group of young disciples who later became monks of the Ramakrishna Order.

Ramakrishna spent most of his life chanting the name of God, writing hymns, kirtans and abhangas.

The following points are prominent in the teachings of Ramakrishna Paramahamsa:

- Life is incomplete without God. God is the basis, shelter and joy of life.

- One should have selfless, fearless and pure devotion towards God. The result of devotion is the sight of God.

- Remembering the name of God and singing his praises is a simple and pleasant way of devotion.

- One must give up everything for God and live according to His will. God's will is best.

- One should serve the devotees of God and remain in their company. Serving devotees is serving God.

- One must respect all religions and know their essence. The goal of all religions is the attainment of God.
- All living beings should be treated equally and compassionately. There is a part of God in all living beings.
- Truth, non-violence, peace, tolerance, humility, purity, penance, faith, prudence, renunciation etc. are the qualities of sadhana. These qualities should be followed.
- There are vices in the world like sorrow, grief, fear, greed, anger, attachment, ego, jealousy, hatred, attachment etc. One should be free from these defects.
- There is nothing without God. God is everything.

Question for Reader

Dear readers, have you ever done self-introspection? If not, then try it by taking out some time from your daily routine and write down your experience on the notes section given at the end of the book.

I am giving below some points which will help you.

- Think about which qualities impress you the most?

- Have you ever sat in meditation posture?

- When did you feel that you had hurt others?

- Which means of eternal happiness would you like to adopt first?

General Yogasana

Day 1

Day 2

Day 3

Day 4

Day 5

General Meditation Posture

Meditation Target Mark Examples

1. Icon

2. Mantra

3. Name-Chanting

राम राम राम राम राम राम

राम राम राम राम राम राम

राम राम राम राम राम राम

राम राम राम राम राम राम

राम राम राम राम राम राम

राम राम राम राम राम राम

राम राम राम राम राम राम

राम राम राम राम राम राम

Daily Yoga Schedule

(30 minutes daily, 3 months)

First month name______________________

1	2	3	4	5	6	7
8	9	10	11	12	13	14
15	16	17	18	19	20	21
22	23	24	25	26	27	28
29	30	31				

(Do ✓ on date after completion of practice)

Daily Yoga Schedule

Daily Yoga Schedule

(30 minutes daily, 3 months)

Second month name__________________

1	2	3	4	5	6	7
8	9	10	11	12	13	14
15	16	17	18	19	20	21
22	23	24	25	26	27	28
29	30	31				

(Do ✓ on date after completion of practice)

Daily Yoga Schedule

Daily Yoga Schedule

(30 minutes daily, 3 months)

Third month name______________________

1	2	3	4	5	6	7
8	9	10	11	12	13	14
15	16	17	18	19	20	21
22	23	24	25	26	27	28
29	30	31				

(Do ✓ on date after completion of practice)

Self Practice Sheets - 2

Daily Meditation Schedule

(10 minutes daily, 3 months)

First month name_______________________

1	2	3	4	5	6	7
8	9	10	11	12	13	14
15	16	17	18	19	20	21
22	23	24	25	26	27	28
29	30	31				

(Do ✓ on date after completion of practice)

Daily Meditation Schedule

(15 minutes daily, 3 months)

Second month name_____________________

1	2	3	4	5	6	7
8	9	10	11	12	13	14
15	16	17	18	19	20	21
22	23	24	25	26	27	28
29	30	31				

(Do ✓ on date after completion of practice)

Daily Meditation Schedule

(20 minutes daily, 3 months)

Third month name________________

1	2	3	4	5	6	7
8	9	10	11	12	13	14
15	16	17	18	19	20	21
22	23	24	25	26	27	28
29	30	31				

(Do ✓ on date after completion of practice)

Tamo Gunas-victory (2 weeks)

Day	Not Got Angry	Not Got arrogant	Donate (by knowledge, hard work, help)
1			
2			
3			
4			
5			
6			
7			
8			
9			
10			

(Do ✓ on date after completion of practice)

Day	Not Got Angry	Not Got arrogant	Donate (by knowledge, hard work, help)
1			
2			
3			
4			
5			
6			
7			
8			
9			
10			

(Do ✓ on date after completion of practice)

Reader Notes

�֍ �֍ ✥ ✣ ✣

* 9 7 9 8 8 8 9 2 7 7 1 0 0 9 *